Interstitials

poems

Interstitials

Caitlin M.S. Buxbaum

Red Sweater Press

P.O. Box 870414
Wasilla, AK 99687
redsweaterpress.com

Copyright © 2020 Caitlin M.S. Buxbaum. All rights reserved.

No part of this book may be used or reproduced in any manner whatsoever without written permission of the publisher except in the case of brief quotations embodied in critical articles and reviews.

Cover and all interior images by the author.

An earlier version of "Pecans" originally appeared in the Winter 2019 edition of *Alaska Women Speak*.

ISBN-13: 978-1-7332677-6-2

Praise for *Interstitials*

"... a joy to spend time with."

— Tara Ballard, poet

"A wide-ranging work, tackling love, loss, partnership, self, family, place, and so many other things. There is much here that speaks to me. More than one poem stopped me in my tracks and made me read again. Not because I didn't understand, but because I wanted to feel it again."

— Dave S. Koster, novelist

"[Reading this book], I found myself in a bubble with Buxbaum, viewing us both through the doors of her poems. Her voice and style are clear and strong as she connects us to the everyday and beyond, from moments of reflection in her own backyard to her travels in Africa. *Interstitials* gives insight to what it means to be a young poet in the 21st century, while reflecting emotional maturity, and challenging the reader to reach that same end."

— Luke Campbell, poet

"Caitlin's latest book of poetry shows you the extraordinary in the ordinary things, drawing from personal, familial and intimate relationships of the past and present. *Interstitials* is a collection that threads together the history, emotion and experience of a lifetime in pieces that I want to share with my own loved ones."

— Heidi Petersen, poet

Praise for *Stakes*

"A wide-ranging slate of interesting and timely topics are beautifully strung together in this book. Each poem feels fresh, like popping a lid off a new jar of jam. One thing that surprised me was the accessibility of religious themes throughout Part IV. As an atheist, I typically don't resonate with these topics, but Caitlin offers a personal window into faith and philosophy that illuminates rather than alienates. A fun read and happy to say I came away from reading it with a long list of favorites!"

– Rebecca Hare, Gustavus alumna

"Self-publishing is not an easy way to go; it involves promoting and publishing your own work, and it takes a skill that not every writer has. But Caitlin is able to do both. [...] When you read her poems, you can kind of imagine some of the questions that undergird them that might come from her training as both a journalist and studying English in college. You can kind of hear the questions down below the surface of the poems, and you can get a sense of the kind of curiosity that either was fed by the journalism experience or maybe the journalism experience fed that curiosity about the world."

– David Cheezem, poet & founder of Fireside Books

Praise for *Uneven Lanes*

"I'm a sucker for the description of love and life as slightly messy, but still agreeable and romantic in spite of it all. To me, this collection of poems captures that sentiment. The poem in this collection that nails it is 'what if instead.' It speaks pure truth to daily married life, the difficulties, and why we cherish it anyhow. This book is worth reading through multiple times."

— Dave S. Koster, novelist

"The poems in *Uneven Lanes* nudge us to see the world in all its complexity, using everyday images — spumoni, for instance — to remind us that what we see or hear might be interpreted in multiple ways. Thus 'a garish-looking flavor' of ice-cream 'sounds more awful / and bewildering / than it tastes' and even 'bad news about a pet dog' can help 'make for an exceptional day / in an ordinary week.' Each of Buxbaum's poems require — gently — that readers seek more than one way to experience their lives. In one of the loveliest poems in the collection, 'what if instead,' the speaker suggests that we seek out what is most beautiful and loving in our lives, so that 'with each line,' as she imagines in '10-4,' we might also practice 'speaking a universal tongue: / Love.'"

— Rebecca Fremo, poet

Other Books by Caitlin M.S. Buxbaum

Songs from the Underground
Ever Unknown, Ever Misunderstood
Uneven Lanes
The Compendium of Lost Poems
Stakes
Wabi-Sabi World: An Artist's Search

*For the fans,
and anyone ever accused
of feeling too much*

Contents

Foreword	xv
Short Timing It	3
Summer	4
Poem for Yesterday	5
Curtis	6
Thank God for Coffee & Beer	7
Chemistry	8
Road Trip	9
Old Friends	13
Wildfire Season	14
Homeless	17
Rumble	18
For Misha: The Actor, The Angel	19
Everything is interesting	20
Place	21
kitchen dancing music	22
After Subbing for a Kindergarten Teacher	23
Witnesses	24
All There Is	27
Congratulations, Goodbye	28
The Patio (Epitaph)	29
Never Alone, Nor Apart	30
To: Mom, After a Date	31
Speechless	32
World	35
There it is again	36
Past, Present, Future (Fingertips)	37
Pecans	38
Tear	40
Scotch Tape	41
ISO	42
My Brother Has No Possessions	43
Reach	47
A new and unpredictable life	48
Uncollected	49

Pockets	50
Banana Peppers	51
Of Persuasion	52
The Power of Poetry	55
Highs and Lows	56
Significant Other	57
At a Poet's Lecture on Tones of Voice	58
Kinyarwanda	59
Rwanda	60
Blessing	63
Tea & Cream	64
How Well I'm Known	65
You, Coffee, Yesterday	66
little lovely moments	69
The Inevitability of Ending	70
My Father's Journal	71

Acknowledgments
About the Author
About the Publisher

Foreword

We're in the midst of a poetic gold rush in Alaska, with so many poets producing great work from all corners of the state. Alaskan poets are more diverse than ever before, and their writing touches on subjects that go beyond the stereotypical alpenglow and aurora-tinted images of the past. Caitlin Buxbaum is a great example. Her poems tackle everything from school lockdowns to the aftermath of genocide in Rwanda, but there's something of her Alaskan upbringing that tints each poem.

I had the privilege of interviewing Caitlin for "What Can Poetry Do?" a radio show and podcast on Palmer's Big Cabbage Radio (radiofreepalmer.org). My co-host, Kenni Psenak Linden, and I discussed Caitlin's work in our September 2019 episode.

With *Interstitials*, Caitlin has produced a poetic collection of "radical innocence." Radical innocence is a willingness to know, to wonder, to imagine. It involves curiosity, awe, courage, and honesty. There's nothing Pollyannaish or naive about it.

I didn't come up with the phrase "radical innocence." I stole it from a poem William Butler Yeats wrote 99 years ago, called, "A Prayer for my Daughter." Yeats writes of his hopes for his daughter's future. Frankly, the poem doesn't age well. It's hard to know when the tender hopes of a father seep into a restrictive paternalism. "May she be granted beauty and yet not / Beauty to make a stranger's eye distraught." Well, that's none of his business, is it?

And I don't know what to do with this: "So let her think opinions are accursed." No opinions? Did he really want his daughter to be so protected from the world, and the world to be protected from his daughter's best thinking?

But Caitlin's poems are radically innocent — even if it's an innocence that Yeats couldn't recognize or value.

I keep thinking about the word "inspire," which appears in several of Caitlin's poems. Here are some lines from "Poem for Yesterday:"

> I saw that same small
> inspired space was
> sheltered beneath the shying
> darkness [...]

"Poem for Yesterday" is wonderfully paradoxical. The move from day to night and from night to day repeats, over and over, but "we can't turn back." We can't return to the shelter of old inspired spaces, but we can cycle on to new ones.

In "Road Trip," the sights and sounds of the road interfere with the pure enjoyment of the music:

> This road has either dulled my senses
> or swallowed up some subtlety of sound
> that lets the listener forget anything
> but the music, the bass beating in your chest,
> the vocal vibrato echoing in your throat,
> the spell-binding synth resonating
> with your uninhibited aura

The last line of the poem — "and I wonder what else I've missed" — leaves open the possibility that the music also interfered with her enjoyment of the ride. We can have one or the other: the music by itself, or the scenery by itself, but try to combine them, and we're stuck in an in-between-state.

Maybe innocence — maybe inspiration — is a lack of clutter.

Most of these poems are bright glimpses of life — a conversation captured here, a moment of wonder captured there, anything that might be considered interstitial. "Everything is interesting," she writes, and her poems bear that out. These are small moments — sometimes funny ones. They haunted me long after I read them, popping up in my mind as I went through my day-to-day life.

These are also poems of courageous intimacy. The poem "Speechless" is so delicate, so loving, so honest.

"My Father's Journal" is more ambitious. In this longer poem, Caitlin records her thoughts as she reads her father's journal from his active duty in a submarine. It's almost as if we can read over her shoulder as she enters the life of her father. We see his unfiltered thoughts, his fears, his lust — all through the eyes of his adult daughter. The speaker doesn't flinch. She takes it in with such grace and equanimity. Near the end of the poem, she includes this line, which is so wonderfully open-ended:

> I have no opinions (yet), only curiosity.

Take that, Mr. Yeats.

David Cheezem

Alaskan poet

founder of Fireside Books

Interstitials

Short Timing It

I
say that
one summer
will only last
as long as there is
love to be had
among thieves
who steal
time

Summer

If May is the month of motorcycles
then June is the juxtaposition
of small dogs in classic cars,
their rolled-down windows
allowing windblown hair
to wave to the beat
of modern punk rock.

This summer is for such
aphorisms & anachronisms,
quieted only by sunshine
and lawn chairs on the porch,
which need no invitation.

The birds would like their privacy,
but the promise of free food
emboldens them enough
to partake in our presence,
and complete the picture
of our personal paradise.

Poem for Yesterday

      and it was like
I had been there before:
one late night/early morning
when the division between
light and dark was
three fingers of gold sky
flattened against the expanse
of rosy gray and bluish gray
and dark stone heavy gray
all in one big heap of cloud

      resting on the horizon
until night collapsed all color.
Then again tonight/today
I saw that same small
inspired space was
sheltered beneath the shying
darkness, folding back its hem
to leave something uncovered
in the light — I can only assume
we can't turn back.

Curtis

A conversation with a dread-locked stranger
(who may or may not have noticed
my wedding ring) and his fetching dog
must be fodder for a poem, which runs on
chance meetings in unfamiliar towns
and imagination gone wild in the summer sun

I'm on my way to Rwanda, I tell him —
he's a traveler, he says,
and a teacher, too, which we agree
doesn't mean what it used to,
doesn't satisfy our innate wanderlust

Words end and we part ways,
to maybe meet again, maybe not —
at least we will have taken
this slim opportunity
to speak our freed minds
without expectation
or judgment.

Thank God for Coffee & Beer

It occurs to me
that the reason we invite people
for coffee or beer
is for want of something
to do with our hands
& mouths
when we ask the big questions
or opinions get controversial
and we either want to reach out
and slap our date across the face
or caress them, propriety be damned.

Thank God for coffee & beer.

Chemistry

Whether you're single or spoken for,
thousands of miles from home or
right in your proverbial backyard,
there's a spark in the air
that surrounds your body
in the midst of attraction,
a tingling sensation that has you hoping
no one can see the fluorescent feeling
emanating from your eye sockets,
has you reasoning,

> *There must be a scientific explanation!*

or else your world will come crashing down,
inflating your heart to impossible proportions
and beating your brain into oblivion —

> *Can you get an aneurysm from infatuation?*

Fear not. You can be comforted, knowing
your "emotions" are actually the body's attempt
to sound the mating call, a series of neuron firings
& glandular fluctuations
designed to get you procreating,
which you recognize will produce
a whole set of other (long-living) problems...

And that sets you walking away, thinking,

> *Of course, it's just science,*

with all the enthusiasm
of a freshman forced to memorize
the periodic table of elements,
learning to live
in a world without magic.

Road Trip

A hundred miles of highway down,
my feet up against the dashboard,
I find myself longing to hear this album
through headphones, or in the comfort
of a quiet room

This road has either dulled my senses
or swallowed up some subtlety of sound
that lets the listener forget anything
but the music, the bass beating in your chest,
the vocal vibrato echoing in your throat,
the spell-binding synth resonating
with your uninhibited aura

       it's all gone, lost in the distance,
and I wonder what else I've missed.

Old Friends

for Mom & Nici

Idle chat about an ocean vessel
brings two maidens back to the glory days,
where the Yukon Bar is the *Puke-on*,
and the Harbor Dining Club is the *How Boring*.
"Might as well cut the gut," they say,
driving down one street and up the other
to cover town in five minutes.

In this century,
around a dwindling campfire,
smiles on suntanned faces
with a little more flesh on them than before
remind me of a generation passed
for a few
         small
              moments.

Wildfire Season

Sitting silently, sunning myself
in these stultifying temperatures,
my mind wanders, eyes closed,
the pleasure of warm, darkening skin
spitting in the face of the wildfires
burning a peninsula down

I shiver as this adulterous heat
steams the gathering clouds,
wilts the house of cards
constructed in my mind
by words exchanged
along telephone lines

I expect to fall
with the changing winds,
& dampen
in the inevitable rain.

Homeless

On a rainy Saturday morning,
I can't shake the sense of irony
from my umbrella of privilege
as I exit the fairgrounds
after a night in a cardboard cave.

Only two days removed from a shower,
donut in hand, I look up just in time to see

HAPPY *AND* HEALTHY

scrolling brightly across the marquee,
as if every truly homeless person
need only stand up and walk
into a happy, healthy life.

I shake my head, climb into my car,
drive home — nothing more, nothing less.

Rumble

The rumble of the road
in rush-hour traffic
as a truck goes by;
the spark of a spent cigarette
skipping along the pavement
in the dark — mild irritations
that prolong the journey
& inspire it, transform it
into something other
than the banal.

I suppose
this is poetry.

For Misha: The Actor, The Angel

You asked for a poem
and I wrote one
in secret, unknown
even to me
but inspired by
you reaching out —
an idol in this world
extending an olive branch,
of sorts: a salve to our ache
for a supernatural connection,
primetime holy water
quenching our salivating psyches,
soothing egos that long to be needed

but at the end of the day
you're just a man
trying to do good
and be loved
like the rest of us

And so what?
Why shouldn't we be the same?
Let these words
and your quest for kindness
be a celebration
of our mutual humanity.

Everything is interesting

Everything is interesting:
watching a bird gliding in flight,
listening to a kid cry & echo itself,
not knowing if it's animal or human;
smelling diesel in the brisk autumn air
biting at your cheeks that redden
in the waning sun, rising wind.
These are the signs of the living,
the created in creation,
interested in everything,
separate but equal
in the most joyous way —
a part of it all.

Place

This must be the place we live in,
where the beautiful people are
the jewelers and real estate agents,
and the uncomely are the ones
on the streets and in the jails

Sometimes I wonder
what would happen
if our places
were reversed.

kitchen dancing music

it's this
kitchen dancing music
that drives my hips
moves my feet
thrills my heart
fills my lungs
with that oxygen alternate
euphoria: joy
in the abandonment
of inhibition

    with the blinds closed
no one else will know
how my bones resound
from this
audial experience
making me a fool
on a Friday afternoon

After Subbing for a Kindergarten Teacher

As I laze
under the weight
of a two-ton headache
(hyperbole warranted)
a dull thought thuds
against my cranium:
will the teacher wonder
what happened
when I stopped
taking notes?
I hope she will
at least appreciate
I sacrificed my sanity
and an afternoon
for hers
and that she will
love her students
a little more
than if she'd
never left
and they will have
forgotten yesterday
forgiven all transgression.

Witnesses

Sometimes I wonder
if our lives are all that inspiring —
can they compare to the half-melted
mountain streams, or the spruce trees
hunched over broken roads in old age?
The tickled screams
of children sliding into lakes,
or the scurrying of little critters
across a virtual highway?

At least we can say
we were witnesses
to it all.

All There Is

In the world of journalism,
nothing is left to chance —
the donuts or breakfast burritos
roll in, the weather comes down,
the telephones ring left and right,
and you know the news is coming in, going out
whether we are there to pick it up, turn it on
or click it open. Something is happening
and the risk is only in seeing
what we choose to see
as all there is.

Congratulations, Goodbye

The "Congratulations!"
for one "You're hired!"
overshadowed by

six months left to live

is enough to make anyone
spell words wrong,
tear tears from their eyes,
and stop caring
for good food. Still,
we dare to hope,
if only because
we've nothing else left to do.

The Patio (Epitaph)

for Jim

Between the paving stones and the cinderblocks,
commingling with dirt, sand and sweat,
swimming in a thick, dark cloud of mosquitoes,
I spotted a small thing called love;
though the body fails, the spirit will not,
and just a hand, or a dozen glazed donuts,
or a carton of cold French fries for the dog,
can remind a person what it means to give,
to build on a foundation, no matter how much
time — life — remains.

Never Alone, Nor Apart

I never thought it alright
to be swollen with soulful happiness
oblivious to all of life's ills
until I found myself beside you
rambling through the misty wilderness
tired & hungry & cold
but willing to take on the world
if only for your love.

Driven on by this thought
I approach our not-too-distant future
when one day
we will never walk alone
nor apart.

To: Mom, After a Date

> "... he makes stupid bets with dangerous people, and when he doesn't pay up, they give him the chop."
>
> — *Snatch* (2000)

If I wrote you a poem,
would you forgive me
for staying out late,
eating chocolate cake
in bed, and using every
sleep-deprived morning
to drink your coffee?
I may be growing up and away
in time and space,
but at least you know:

I've made no "stupid bets
with dangerous people," and
we only watched a movie.

Speechless

As we lay there in the dark
I noticed your voice
moving with the deep rhythms
of the music, my whispers evaporating
in the invisible tenor trails
ribboning through the air
like an imagined aurora,
no hope of being heard in the color.

Then again, perhaps it was better
to be thought and rendered silent
by that soft blanket of sounds,
than to risk words which could spoil
the moment, and fail to show you
how speechless your body makes me.

Lover, do not forget the awe
with which I always see you.

World

You were reading to your nephew
about dragons and tacos
when I noticed something —
not the way he teetered
on the edge of the sofa,
as Grandma pointed out,
or how your sister tried to know me,
across a poor connection,
or how many foam neon balls
lay scattered throughout the living room,
after being fired in a great and terrible battle...

       it was how still and slow the world was,
even as the little blonde boy giggled, the T.V.
chattered, and the dogs & cats wandered about;
how his eyes & mine followed yours
when you were the center of it all.

There it is again

There it is again
that noise
that doubt
that fear
grinding into static
breaking with a want ad:

Artist, Female, Seeking Approval

in the absence of your voice.

Without it, I withdraw
as I assume
you're listening
always
and not answering

Past, Present, Future (Fingertips)

The peeling fingertips on my left hand
say so much about me — sure
I'm into folk music, rock 'n' roll even,
but what else can you see?
The attempts to make a habit of something
that takes more patience than I often have?
The cyclical pursuit & abandonment of dreams?
It's procrastination, at least — avoidance, too —
that leads to these rough edges
I continually work to smooth out

Then again, I guess
these ravaged fingertips
complete the portrait
of this past & present me
I keep dying to see, draped
in the fashion of Dorian Gray

God forbid I learn the truth about myself
before the appointed time, or it's too late

Pecans

On the dining room floor in the house my dad built
there's a box
half-full of close-to-rotten pecans, and mostly full
of broken pecan shells.

I want to make it symbolic, but really, we're all just
too lazy to sort out the good ones,
and no one has the heart to throw them all away. Maybe

they would've made a great pie
or two
or three —

if we'd had enough stamina to shell them all
in the week after they'd been gifted to us,
to press on through the thumb-blisters and the build-up
of bitter shell residue that promised an inner sweetness which,
to be honest, usually didn't amount to anything;

or else we ate the fruit before it made it
into the pie-fund pile.

So now the box is still sitting there, beneath the windowsill,
among the clutter,
like it was born to be there. It's become a fixture
of the room, or the floor,
for no reason other than its insignificance, a part of
the collection of unmemorable memorabilia.

Maybe it would mean something to somebody. But
in our house,
it's just a cardboard box. Full of nuts and their shells.

And when it's gone, no one will notice, because
everything else will probably be gone too,
and all the heirlooms and birth certificates and trophies will

take precedence, in the preservation process

because expensive hand-me-downs, "maiden" names
— who assumes such virtue anymore? —
and evidence of someone besides us losing a game
cause more fuss about where they should be stored
than a box of pecans.

Eventually, they'll be thrown out, I suppose,
never offered the opportunity to be properly disposed of,
after careful consideration:

> *Should we save these?*
> *Nah, just throw 'em out.*

And that would be it. Anything could've been in that box.

Tear

I keep thinking about
that tear in your eye,
the one that beaded up
on your cheek,
showed itself in one
moment of weakness,
lovely and fleeting.

If I am ever graced by
that manifestation of
trust again, I should
count myself luckier
than any human being
who has been asked,
as gently as a mother
waking her child,
to please rise, and meet
the love of their life.

Scotch Tape

"It's like Velcro, or Scotch Tape," he says,
peeling his body off of mine.

"Scotch Tape," I muse, "That's pretty difficult
to pull apart."

He smiles and says, "I know."
I tell us not to get ahead of ourselves.

But when he leans into me again,
ahead of ourselves no longer seems so far away;

I've forgotten what there is to worry about,
in love.

ISO

It's the clearest metaphor for
compensation — the higher you go,
the more you push the limits,
the more it shows in the end result.

See that grain, the speckled stains of
artificially lightened pixels?
that's the sign of sacrifice,
whether forced or reasoned.

Only the capture of a moment,
too important to leave behind,
can justify the decision made
by the photographer's hand.

My Brother Has No Possessions

for Joyce Sutphen

My brother has no possessions,
not a single piece of furniture, or a stereo,
to his name. As he wanders through
the equatorial countries of South America,
I wonder if he remembers
that one photograph
pinned to my bulletin board,
where he is chucking a stone
at me, the photographer, more focused
on capturing his likeness
than paying attention
to whatever is coming my way.

Reach

The instinct to reach
for my camera
when I see a bumblebee
and a butterfly
feasting on my garden
reminds me: Lately
I haven't had enough
quiet moments
to just be still and
enjoy the ephemeral

A new and unpredictable life

It's the smell of old-timey sophistication
that stops me, reminds me I am involved
in an art spanning generations and more,
flooded with memories of people who don't
share timelines; perhaps it is this travel
through the years that puts ideas in our heads
which have been written before, but only
through a lens different enough from our own
it gains a new and unpredictable life

Uncollected

after Allen Ginsberg

your poems
my thoughts
this world
& all its problems
compiled but not
collected
form a darker sense of doom
than you could imagine
in death;
in life,
we still burn with wonder
warmed by your limelight
reflecting
then directing
us through time
& that world,
your thoughts
our poems
uncollected.

Pockets

If only I were more like
my tiny, useless pockets:
unable to hold anything
that isn't small, light, or
otherwise un-burdensome —
anything that doesn't belong.

Banana Peppers

rain down on the counter-top in acidic yellow, scattering loops on the floor, a match-on-action with the perfect Os of surprise forming in the mouths of petrified bystanders

one "Oh my goodness!" rotates my body and suddenly adrenaline co-opts my hands, flinging that bright debris from this woman's body, shoving her shoulders aside to keep the vomit from filling her lungs, kicking myself for forgetting her name (as if it made a difference) and *no one is coming* and *we are alone* and *wait it's stopping*, "Sabrina..."

She wipes the dark, slimy substance from her face, stares at me in stock, wide-eyed terror, and I reply, "It's okay," see the peace and truth of those words accepted, reflected in the calm of her eyes, which neither the supervisors nor the medics notice when they ask the girl in the vegetables if she knows what day it is

"Just so you know," she says, having passed their test, "the fainting runs in my family."

Of Persuasion

> "... these were noises which belonged to the winter pleasures; her spirits rose under their influence; and ... after being long in the country, nothing could be so good for her as a little quiet cheerfulness."
>
> from Persuasion by Jane Austen
1818

Slush and steam: sounds of winter, outside and inside, onomatopoetic but unrecognized by the masses, until they hear the hissing and the squishing and the art of getting through a December day, Alaska beating to the stretch of its own drum around the fire and ice and everything nice but not so much as the quiet, the little quiet, small with comfort and lack of conversation, though it isn't all bad when you consider what cheer the season brings, even as the snow sinks softly through the thick air, air thick with feeling and spirit instead of words, until someone's broken the ice, for better or worse, tasting the sounds of socked-in solstice with their cherry tongue, with pleasure, sniffing at something unsaid, unheard in the long-lost country; if a snowflake falls in the meadow, has climate change turned the world upside down, on its head, whatever that means in the vast expanse of the universe, filled with stars and galaxies like so much cosmic slush and steam, an inside-out song of shared space?

It is written: These are the indelible and effortless marks of a momentary, solitary, persuasion.

The Power of Poetry

for David Cheezem & Kenni Linden

When my pen moves ahead of my thoughts,
or vice versa, and "readers" has turned to "poetry,"
I smile at my beautiful mistake, equating people
with words so pretty, so poignant, so provocative,
they needed a name; one can only hope
those individuals who read, confused with art,
live up to such potential, and become that
which inspires, loves, yearns, moves,
breathes life into the soul —

such is the power of poetry.

Highs and Lows

At a poetry reading — buzzed
on a single glass of pinot noir that
stains my self-conscious lips,
working hard to not be antisocial —
I'm swimming in words I do not hear,
inscrutable sounds that pierce this
uncommon humidity,
without specificity

What is it that makes us poets
afraid of other people, and also
desirous of community, of validation?
What is this solitude we crave
and then abhor?

In answer, watch
as I subject myself
to this agony again,
in the heat of a record high,
and believe anew
in the power of people
I don't want to know, but must —
perhaps already do.

Significant Other

Bless my pink and tired husband
flush from libations and
the exertion of being social
contrary to his reclusive tendencies;
it takes a special person
to brave a crowd of strangers
and endure the waxing of words,
waning of artistry,
for the sake of one's
significant other.

At a Poet's Lecture on Tones of Voice

What if
these encroaching fits of musicality
as Cedar Sigo said
are all we poets have
from the beginning
and at the end
of our struggling orchestrated existence?
Whatever future we sing of
whatever Fate is plucking the strings
perhaps our words are all we need
to sustain beauty
find inner peace
and it will (have to) be enough.

Kinyarwanda

for Elvis

Following a T or an S, an H in the mouth
of a Rwandan speaking English
is like an accident waiting to happen,
an undeployed airbag to protect the speaker
from the potential pile-up of letters to come,
later proven dysfunctional, with a hissing deflation.

But try a T after an initial N in his language
and he'll laugh (hopefully internally) at your attempt
to master sounds that don't exist, or don't
belong to you, and maybe can't, never will.

And the K? After an interior N, absent;
before an I, it could be the precursor to
an explosion, like the pin-pull of a grenade
or the cocking of a loaded gun, albeit not
one aimed to kill (though maybe to confuse).

But don't get me started on the W.
After an R or a B, it either disappears
or brings a G along for the ride, and good luck
getting that guttural sound right — what glides
off his tongue comes out like a vomit of sounds
from an uncouth American mouth.

Even still I make the effort, if only to understand
fidelity, in a new-but-old language.

Rwanda

Here, incandescent light shines
through shards of broken glass
guarding a house of prayer
like holy fires burning low,
brightening the murky night.
Even the tiniest embers
make a way through the darkness,
just as the smallest countries
find peace in anguish,
hope in despair, and grace
in the face of betrayal.

Let us learn from the ones
who have lost too much,
risen higher than we would
in our seals of security,
for what little of theirs remains
is more than we could bear.

Blessing

    for Sandrali

Having what might be considered
Rwanda's most famous architect and holy man
make us pour-over coffee in his posh African home
humbles my heart in a way that makes me feel like royalty.

What could my company be worth, that it would warrant
such a blessing? I imagine it's more between him and God,
than him and me. Whatever the case, in this moment,
I will listen to anything he has to say.

Tea & Cream

I'm not British,
but it's something about me,
you think,
that's well represented
by tea & cream. I wonder
if I'll ever live up to
the refined simplicity,
sweet mystery,
or warm charity
of such a drink,
as I imagine it to be.

How Well I'm Known

    I'm talking to my husband across the room
    when a reflexive yelp escapes my lips,
    as the book of poetry I've been reading
    shutters itself against my will.
    "Lost your page, didn't ya?" he asks,
    unseeing, and I smile at his recognition
    of this infinitesimal tragedy, which
    shows me just how well I'm known.

You, Coffee, Yesterday

Rolling around my floorboard
is an almost empty coffee cup,
enough liquid left to make a mess —
it came from yesterday, not long before I met you
in the thick of shadowed misery, masked
by gin and Quinn and maraschino cherries
(and your funky folk singing, too).

It was lovely, and tragic.

Then I made my way homeward,
ignoring the stains from last night
until this morning, when I looked at
your life, and imagined what he'd taken from you,
saw the almost empty memory of him
rolling around in your sweetened, swimming head,
enough love left to make a mess.

It was sublime, elegiac.

And here we are now, laughing
in the throes of sticky friendship,
enough of that "us" to make a mess
of my life, if I'm not careful and ever conscious
of the almost empty space in which we
might forget ourselves, rolling around in
(and under) our own influence.

That's the danger, the magic.

little lovely moments

i wasn't the first
to name them —
these little lovely
moments — but i
noticed, in the
timbre of her voice
& the wet kisses of
that smiling child,
what you felt
in a rare embrace
from your best
friend, and saw
in his eyes:
the weight of
these little lovely
moments, tipping
the ancient scales
to a softer, more
hopeful world.

The Inevitability of Ending

And there it was
hanging in the silence:
the inevitability of ending,
a death
unspeakable, but imminent.

We wait
for the moment to pass,
and the understanding between us
to change —

you watch a loved one perish
and I let you fall
into my arms,
comforting, but feeling nothing

save your aching heartbeat
moving mine
to the rhythm of your loss.

My Father's Journal

I.
Before I have even opened the book in my hands,
I sense I possess something sacred, a known name
scrawled across the top, doodles inked below
in a familiar style (the kind I used to watch him
create in church services and business meetings
when I was a child): dashed lines along the spine
and geometric shapes carefully contained
within four, fluid, amoeba-like homes —
those cells and squares aren't going anywhere.

This faded, verdant, cloth-bound record may be
all that's left, someday, of a certain part of history
that won't seem significant to some,
but means so much to me.

Inside, I don't understand the drawings, but I know
they're not the absent-minded wanderings of the cover;
something more predictable, mechanical, functional —
circuits, perhaps ("mobiles," he tells me later).

And then there are the pages — two, it appears,
have been ripped out, and I can't tell if it's
disappointment or excitement welling up in me,
wondering when the removal took place. But
before I can ponder any longer, I'm distracted
by the date — no year — on the present paper,
and the metaphor of a flat horse that amuses me;
was he trying to be cool, or was this
the standard slang of the day?

As I read on, I'm astonished to find myself
poring over poetry, something I never expected
to see in a submarine. And ere I've had time
to marvel, delight, truly process
the stylized words before me,

I am sunk into the emotional depths of despair
caused by the realization, "Nobody listens,"
followed by self-doubt and a slip into the script
rarely used today, and never so neatly
by a 20-something male, anymore.

II.
It's the punctuated "Fuck." at the end — in print —
that hooks me. Cursive is all his hand knows now,
aside from that. And then there's the love, even
sensuality, not for my mother. These are revelations
from an era outside of me, beyond and before
in a way that means I can never truly know it.

III.
The fear, viscerally rendered by the two torpedoes,
is as real as the aftermath, in which war is made
a memory, so quickly and comically it makes him
angry, and me too. Don't they know? Don't they care?
We both know the answer, or think we do.

IV.
Offshore, but headed back to sea, I feel the
brokenness of his hands, and the bitterness
of leaving his loved one behind — not
that he would ever want her with him
in that god-forsaken prison, but that
the stress of his pending "duty" and
separation from his bride-to-be
is already showing on his skin.

V.
"Variables," he says, in an attempt at "brighter thoughts"
that seems almost forced, are what constitute life —
the "contrast" between discipline of the mind &
volatility of emotion, pragmaticism & dreams.
This young man has not met God, but he is not wrong
when he says, "Even death is life."

VI.
"I am my originality." I don't understand it
until he compares his self-proclaimed gift
to the art of a painter, or sculptor, or writer;
he doesn't know it yet, but he is a beautiful creation
blessed (and cursed?) with thoughts that trouble
other people as much as entertain. He asks
his followers to "let go" of their fears and
"come with me," not hearing Jesus in his words,
or considering why he changed his name to Paul.

VII.
Anger. Rage. The urge to fight, unprovoked.
He doesn't say it, but I see the red in his eyes,
feel the rattle in his bones, the venom on his
breath, the growl in his chest, the boiling of
his blood — I've seen it before, in him and
in me. Maybe this is where it started —
"Suppression."

I feel the necessity of forgiveness
and pity for fools.

VIII.
Keep your cards close to your chest, my husband
always says, and I comprehend how different
his heritage is from mine, which talks of being
outspoken and punished by stupidity incarnate
for seeking truth in the opening of one's mouth,
in the irresistible showing of one's hand.

Suppression — there it is again.

The decision to be silent
is no less combustible
than the one to speak.

IX.
Duty be damned — he needs to see her.
Is paranoid, but knowledgeable (about
what, I don't know). Falls in love, again
and again, but maybe not with the same
woman, maybe not in the present.

He thinks there will be no plateau
with Mary Beth, but I know better.

Still, I can't tell him.

X.
Over, finished as it's barely begun,
with notes of months, maybe years,
gone by in the form of slides inventoried
for storage — prints and negatives of pets,
a wedding, plants, and a place I can't
pronounce, then more of the same, though
"Vanilla Fudge & Jimi Hendrix" stands out,
along with the play I already know
from the stories that aren't secret:
"Very good," he notes.

At least three quarters of the journal is empty,
and I can't help but wonder why (though
I've been guilty of the same), and want to
inquire after a sequel. This slim volume
opens such a wide window, but
it is not enough. I hunger for "the rest"
without considering what it might cost.
I have no opinions (yet), only curiosity,
and a longing for a life lost, but only just.

Perhaps this sliver of the past
has many more to be added to it,
to sketch a clearer picture of a reality
that seems unreal, as my own writings

may do one day, for another who writes
a poem about a parent's journal.

Like this book? Review it! Go to amzn.to/38DuAI7 to review on Amazon or bit.ly/2rLdxDr to review on Goodreads, or simply tell your friends to check it out! Spread the word however you like, just remember: Be specific, be honest, and be fair.

Acknowledgments

I am incredibly proud of this book, and that is in large part due to the support of many friends, family members, mentors, colleagues and even strangers who have shown an interest in my work.

In writing, I'd like to thank the following people and entities, in no particular order: my dad, my husband, my mom, my dad's cousin Linda, Mitchell Davidson, Adam Mackie, David Cheezem, Heidi Petersen, Rebecca Fremo, Rebecca Hare, Poetry Parley, The Writer's Block Bookstore & Café, Luke Campbell, the cast and fans of Supernatural, Kelly Dau, Hannah Bulovsky, Kimberly Jackson-Matta & her husband Matthew, Ben Wargo, my mom's cousin Sally, my mother-in-law Bonnie and sister-in-law Tina, Wendy Brooker, Dave S. Koster, and Taylor Jordan at Black Birch Books. All of you make this accidental passion of mine possible.

Thank you.

About the Author

Caitlin M.S. Buxbaum (also known as Cait Buxbaum) is a poet, teacher, photographer and "former" journalist born and raised in Alaska. She has a Master of Arts in Teaching Secondary English from University of Alaska Anchorage and a Bachelor of Arts in Japanese Studies and English with an emphasis in Creative Writing from Gustavus Adolphus College. She wrote more than 600 stories in three years as a reporter for the *Mat-Su Valley Frontiersman* and has had work featured in *Alaska Women Speak*, among other literary magazines. This is her seventh book from Red Sweater Press.

Follow her on Twitter & Instagram @caitbuxbaum
or visit her website at caitbuxbaum.com

About the Publisher

Once upon a time, when the author of this book first started to think of herself as a writer, there was a red hooded sweatshirt she wore every day — or at least, near enough to every day, that she would become known for it by her friends.

As middle school wore on, and high school came around the bend, the red sweatshirt — affectionately and more conveniently known as the Red Sweater — made fewer and fewer appearances in public, its cuffs having almost completely separated from the arms. Still, it was too big for its owner — she would never be able to fill it.

And so, it came to rest in storage.

But the sweatshirt wasn't forgotten. It lay safely enshrined in a plastic tote, tucked under old yearbooks and framed photos from years gone by, in a warm, wooden shed.

In its current, more abstract incarnation for Red Sweater Press, the red hooded sweatshirt represents that lingering desire for the past, that holding onto of sentimentality and identity, as well as the cultivation of mystery, and perhaps the sense that somewhere along the line, something dramatic happened — and the story didn't end there.

These are the ideas behind Red Sweater Press, which reflect the kind of stories this company aims to publish.

We hope you enjoy everything Red Sweater Press has to offer, now and for many years to come.

Follow us on Facebook & Instagram: @redsweaterpress

www.ingramcontent.com/pod-product-compliance
Lightning Source LLC
Chambersburg PA
CBHW042118100526
44587CB00025B/4105